2001

JURASSIC PARK III

Dino expert, Dr. Alan Grant is tricked by a couple into joining a rescue mission to save their son Eric who has disappeared on Isla Sorna. The mission goes badly and Dr. Grant ends up being stalked by a scary Spinosaurus and needing rescuing himself.

Lesson learned:
Don't mess with nature. It's bigger than us and may just bite back!

Lesson learned:
It's hard to get off the island alive.

2015

JURASSIC WORLD

More than 20 years after the original theme park failed, Jurassic World is now open for business. Big business! But when top asset Indominus rex escapes containment and goes on a killing spree, it's not just the visitors who are in danger, but the dinosaurs themselves.

Human Heroes

While the incredible dinosaurs are undeniably the stars of the show, several human characters have also left their mark on Isla Nublar, thanks to their heroic deeds and brave behaviour.

JOHN HAMMOND

Role: Owner of InGen and cloner of dinosaurs

Loves: dinosaurs

Dislikes: anyone who wants to shut down his park

Most likely to: not consider the consequences of manipulating nature

Heroic action: turning his dream of a dinosaur park into reality

DR. ALAN GRANT

Role: Paleontologist

Loves: digging up fossils

Most likely to: save you from a dinosaur attack

Least likely to: underestimate a dinosaur's killer instincts

Heroic action: protects Tim and Lex from the dinosaurs and keeps them safe

DR. IAN MALCOLM

Role: Super-brain Mathematician

Likes to: give his opinion

Most likely to: predict doom and gloom for the future of the park

Least likely to: hide the truth

Heroic action: bravely saves San Diego from a rampaging Tyrannosaurus rex

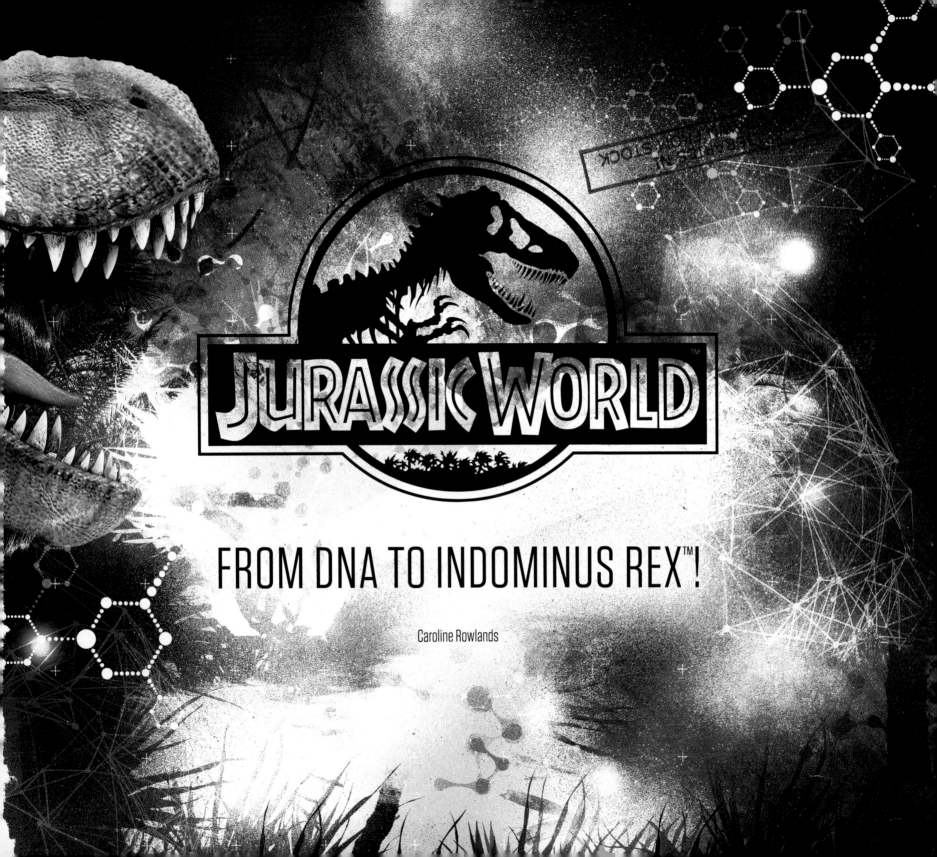

JURASSIC WORLD™

FROM DNA TO INDOMINUS REX™!

Caroline Rowlands

The Age of Jurassic

The deadly dinos at Isla Nublar theme park have given us plenty of thrills and gory blood spills. There's been a dramatic new dino DNA discovery to enthral us too! Before we embark on our Jurassic journey, let's take a moment to remember the story so far...

1993

JURASSIC PARK

John Hammond's dinosaur dream turns to a nightmare when his newly created theme park on Isla Nublar suffers a security failure before it even opens. Dinosaurs escape, guests are munched, all in all, not a good start.

Lesson learned:
T. rex doesn't want to be fed. He wants to hunt!

1997

THE LOST WORLD: JURASSIC PARK II

Years later, Hammond reveals he has also been busy breeding dinosaurs on another island called Isla Sorna. Dino hunters invade the island to capture the prehistoric beasts and transport them to a zoo. This turns out rather badly for everyone involved.

Lesson learned:
Taking dinosaurs off the island was the worst idea in a long, sad history of bad ideas!

CLAIRE DEARING

Role: Operations Manager of the park

Likes to: be in charge

Dislikes: chaos

Most likely to: forget dinosaurs are living creatures

Heroic action: shows brains and courage in releasing Tyrannosaurus rex to defeat Idomninus rex

DR. ELLIE SATTLER

Role: Paleobotanist (studies the evolutionary history of plants)

Likes: dinosaurs and plant fossils

Dislikes: being chased by dinosaurs

Most likely to: work out what a dinosaur has eaten by studying its poop

Heroic action: gets the power back on in the park, reactiviating the protective fences

OWEN GRADY

Role: Dinosaur Trainer and Researcher

Respects: dinosaurs

Dislikes: authority

Most likely to: save the day

Heroic action: shows loyalty and respect to his Raptor team, who in return protect him from Indominus rex

9

GYROSPHERE VALLEY

GOLF COURSE

BOTANICAL GARDENS

GONDOLA LIFT

FERRY LANDING

HOTEL COMPLEX

GENTLE GIANTS PETTING ZOO

TRICERATOPS TERRITORY

T. REX KINGDOM

MOSASAURUS FEEDING SHOW

GALLIMIMUS VALLEY

CRETACEOUS CRUISE

THE AVIARY

BAMBOO FOREST

Go Exploring!

The time-defying Jurassic World is where, for the first time in history, dinosaurs old and new roam together and humans can get up close and personal – if they dare!

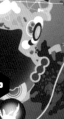

FAMILY FUN

Bursting with amazing attractions, thrilling rides and prehistoric fun, the theme park at Isla Nublar is a holiday experience like no other. There's even a world-class golf course, beautiful gardens and a wild water park!

DINO ZONES

Guests are able to interact with both gentle giants and fierce hunter dinosaurs alike in these star attraction dino zones.

3. Mosasaurus Feeding Show:
You won't forget the sight of the Mosasaurus snapping up its lunch! Warning: you will get wet!

5. Hammond Creation Lab:
Where astonishing scientists at Jurassic World bring prehistoric beasts back to life.

2. T. Rex Kingdom:
Dare to get close to the terrifying Tyrannosaurus rex in this ever-popular attraction.

4. The Aviary and Pteranodon Peak:
Look to the skies to enjoy the world's only flying pterosaurs. For the best views head to Pteranodon Peak.

1. Gyrosphere:
Experience dinosaurs sleeping, eating and roaming in their natural habitat!

ACTIVATION PAGE

Take control of the
Gyrosphere!
Open the app on your mobile device and view these pages.

The Living Tank!

Paleontologists call this tough dinosaur the living tank as its chunky body is so well protected with spiky armour and a deadly tail.

UP CLOSE

Visitors to the park can enjoy these tough plant-eaters on the Gyropshere tour. Advanced technology will prevent anyone from venturing too close, as making an Ankylosaurus feel threatened can be lethal.

WARRIOR WEAPONS

The Ankylosaurus' main weapon is its strong and heavy tail which it swings around to ward off predators. Strong enough to break bones, it would have come in handy back in the Cretaceous period, when Ankylosaurus lived alongside Tyrannosaurus rex.

DISCOVERY

Famous dino hunter Barnum Brown led the team which discovered Ankylosaurus fossils in Montana, USA in 1906.

ARMOUR PLATED

From the fused bones of its hard skull down to the rounded club at the end of its tail, an Akylosaurus is built for protection. Indominus rex soon finds its weak spot though and wastes no time in tossing its victim over and sinking its teeth into its soft, unprotected tummy.

ACTIVATION PAGE

Release the warrior **Ankylosaurus** with your mobile device by opening the app and viewing these pages.

Ankylosaurus

Lived:	Cretaceous (68 to 66 million years ago), in North America and now, in Jurassic World
Eats:	plants
Length:	7 m long
Speed:	up to 24 km/h
Movie sightings:	*Jurassic Park III* and *Jurassic World*

You are here:

Massive Munchers

The ginormous plant-eating dinosaurs known as Sauropods are truly colossal and easy to recognize thanks to their long necks, even longer tails and chunky bodies.

BIG EATERS

Sauropods like Apatosaurus, Diplodocus and Brachiosaurus are herbivores that feast on plants. They have blunt teeth, good for stripping leaves off trees, and they swallow stones (called gastroliths) to help grind the leaves up in their tummies.

STRONG STOMPERS

The word Sauropod means 'lizard foot' and these big beasts first appeared in the Triassic period about 200 million years ago. They roamed everywhere and fossils have been found on all continents including Antarctica.

DID YOU KNOW?

Apatosaurus is one of the largest animals ever to walk on earth . It's as long as two buses and as heavy as four African elephants.

WHIP WEAPON

Dino experts believe Sauropods use their long tails to help balance their bodies and also as a whip-like weapon to ward off predators.

Apatosaurus

Lived:	Jurassic (150 million years ago) in the USA and now, in Jurassic World
Eats:	plants
Length:	27.5 m long
Weight:	36,000 kg
Speed:	up to 8 km/h
Movie sightings:	*Jurassic World*

You are here:

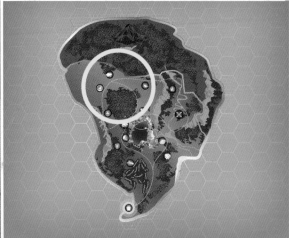

Thick Headed

The odd-looking Pachycephalosaurus is a big hit with visitors to the park, who can enjoy extraordinary sightings of this tough dino in action in the Pachy Arena.

TOUGH NUT

Its thick dome skull is almost 25 cm thick in parts and covered in small knobs, making it perfect for a spot of head butting. This comes in very handy when it's under attack or wants to prove its dominance in the herd.

HAPPY HERD

A Pachycephalosaurus roams happily in a herd, much like a modern-day buffalo although it walks on two, rather than four legs. Owen Grady worries that its head-butting antics will short out its implant and make the herd hard to track.

Pachycephalosaurus

Lived:	Cretaceous (70 to 66 million years ago) in North America and now, in Jurassic World
Eats:	plants
Length:	5 m long
Movie sightings:	*The Lost World: Jurassic Park II* and *Jurassic World*

You are here:

Flying Killers

Jurassic World's enclosed Aviary enables the world's only living pterosaurs to soar and glide high above the park, demonstrating their amazing flying and hunting skills.

HIGH FLIERS

The Pteranodons are the park's biggest pterosaurs. They have a wider wingspan than any known bird. They are primarily fish-eaters, but when a crashing helicopter smashes a hole in the Aviary roof, they start pecking at the guests too.

SNAPPY ATTACKER

It's easy to tell a Pteranodon from other pterosaurs thanks to its short tail and the crest on its head. A Pteranodon's beak is toothless, which is unlike earlier pterosaurs but similar to modern-day birds.

Pteranodon

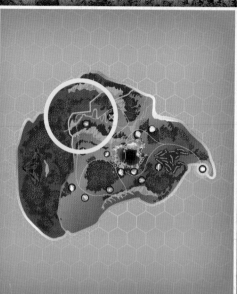

Lived:	Cretaceous (around 88–82 million years ago) in USA and Europe and now, in Jurassic World
Eats:	fish
Wingspan:	7.6 m
Weight:	30 kg
Movie sightings:	*The Lost World: Jurassic Park II, Jurassic Park III* and *Jurassic World*

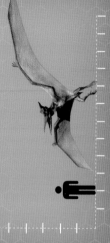

You are here:

DID YOU KNOW?

With its powerful wings and soaring ability, the Pteranodon's range outside the Aviary would extend over 1,500 km, enabling it to hunt far off Isla Nublar given the chance.

FELLOW FLYER

Dimorphodon is the park's other pterosaur species. It originally soared through Jurassic skies with quick snappy jaws and sharp teeth. Smaller than a Pteranodon, with a wingspan of around 1.8 m, it has large eyes to help it seek out prey.

ACTIVATION PAGE

Release the swooping **Pteranodon** with your mobile device by opening the app and viewing these pages.

Tyrant Lizard

One of the deadliest carnivores to walk on the planet, Tyrannosaurus rex dominated its territory more than 60 million years ago and is the star attraction at Jurassic World, until Indominus rex threatens its crown!

SHARP STABBERS

A Tyrannosaurus rex has up to 60 teeth in its huge jaws and sharp stabbing claws, which all help it capture, kill then eat its prey. Experts believe it can eat up to 230 kg of meat in one bite.

STAR ATTRACTION

One of the fiercest predators at Jurassic World, the Tyrannosaurus rex has existed on Isla Nublar for more than 25 years.

DID YOU KNOW?

A Tyrannosaurus rex's brain has a large part devoted to its sense of smell. So even if it can't see its prey, it can always smell it.

Tyrannosaurus rex

Lived:	Cretaceous (68 to 66 million years ago) in North America and now, in Jurassic World
Eats:	meat
Length:	13.4 m long
Speed:	up to 29 km/h
Movie sightings:	*Jurassic Park, The Lost World: Jurassic Park II, Jurassic Park III* and *Jurassic World*

KING KILLER

This meat-eating monster saves the day when she bravely battles Indominus rex, with a little help from her Raptor buddies, proving she's worthy of her title tyrant lizard king.

You are here:

ACTIVATION PAGE

Release the ferocious **Tyrannosaurus rex** with your mobile device by opening the app and viewing these pages.

Hunting Pack

Small but deadly, Jurassic World's Raptors show true cunning and bravery as they battle together as a pack of ferocious fighters.

TERROR TEAM

Owen Grady imprinted on Charlie, Delta, Blue and Echo soon after they were created in the Creation Lab, which enabled him to train them. These predatory dinos are both vicious and smart and learned an amazing 40 different commands during their training.

ALPHA ATTRACTION

The Raptors are the most intelligent predators created in the Creation Lab. Always on the hunt, they look to Owen as their Alpha until Indominus rex seizes command and lures them on her trail of destruction across Isla Nublar.

DID YOU KNOW?

The Raptors have 15-cm curved razor-sharp claws on each hand, perfect for slashing their victims with.

DINO DISCOVERY

The terror team at Jurassic World would not have been possible if it weren't for the fossil discoveries of the past. The first Velociraptor fossil was named in 1924 by Henry Osborn. Some dinosaur experts believe Velociraptors may have been covered in feathers, not scales.

Velociraptor

Lived:	Cretaceous (75 to 71 million years ago) in Mongolia and China and now, in Jurassic World
Eats:	meat
Length:	3.9 m long (and 1.7 m tall)
Speed:	up to 39 km/h
Movie sightings:	*Jurassic Park, The Lost World: Jurassic Park II, Jurassic Park III* and *Jurassic World.*

You are here:

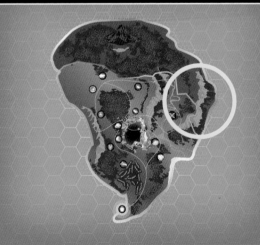

Release the vicious
Velociraptor
with your mobile device by opening the app and viewing these pages.

JURASSIC WORLD
ISLA NUBLAR
Lagoon
HOME OF MOSASAURUS

Snappy Swimmer

The fearsome Mosasaurus once ruled the prehistoric seas and is now the star water attraction in the Jurassic World lagoon.

BIG BITE

A Mosasaurus has huge, sharp teeth in its upper jaw to ensure any prey sliding down its throat won't be able to escape. Its hinged jaw also allows this giant sea lizard to swallow prey larger than its head.

DID YOU KNOW?

The komodo dragon and monitor lizards are among the closest living relatives of the Mosasaurus.

Mosasaurus

Lived: Cretaceous (70 to 66 million years ago) and now, in Jurassic World

Eats: fish, sharks, birds, other marine life and the odd human when it gets the chance!

Length: 22 m long

Weight: up to 20,000 kg

Movie sightings: *Jurassic World*

You are here:

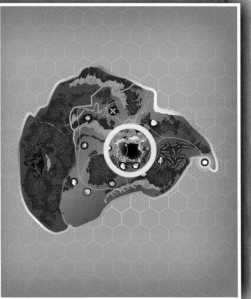

POWERFUL PREDATOR

Mosasaurus lurches up out of the water when it senses prey close by, snapping pterosaurs (and humans) from the air. Even the mighty Indominus rex is no match for this colossal creature. Indominus rex is dragged by Mosasaurus' wide snapping jaw to its grisly death at the bottom of the lagoon.

ACTIVATION PAGE

Let the splash-tastic **Mosasaurus** loose with your mobile device by opening the app and viewing those pages.

Super Snapper

The scary Spinosaurus has a long narrow jaw, just like a crocodile's, which is perfect for snapping up prey, both in and out of the water.

LOST IN BATTLE

Amazing Spinosaurus fossils were discovered in Egypt in the early 1900s, but they were destroyed by bombs during World War II.

DID YOU KNOW?

Spinosaurus lived in tropical lagoons, where giant fish up to 3 m long would have been its prey.

VICIOUS CLAWS

With three claws on each hand, including a long thumb claw, the Spinosaurus stabs and snaps at its enemies and victims.

STRANGE SAIL

Its easy to spot a Spinosaurus thanks to the large sail on its back. Paleontologists are not totally sure what it was for. It could have been used to help control its temperature by catching sunlight to warm up its blood, or as a device to scare off attacking dinosaurs.

Spinosaurus

Lived:	Cretaceous (112 to 95 million years ago) in North Africa and recently on Isla Sorna
Eats:	meat and fish
Length:	18 m long
Speed:	32 km/h
Movie sightings:	*Jurassic Park III*

You are here:

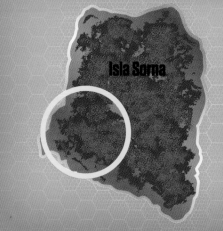

Isla Sorna

ACTIVATION PAGE

Release the awesome **Spinosaurus** with your mobile device by opening the app and viewing these pages.

Super Science

Jurassic World's geneticists set out to create the most fearsome dinosaur ever. With the Indominus rex they more than delivered.

BIGGER, BETTER, BADDER!

Funded by InGen mastermind Simon Masrani, Idominus rex was not bred, she was designed in the Hammond Creation Lab. At first glance, she resembles a T. rex, but her ultra-tough body has been created by complicated genetically modified DNA from Therapods known as Abelisaurs. Her horns are above her eye orbits and come from genetic material from Carnataurs, Majungasaurus, Rugops and Gigantosaurus.

DID YOU KNOW?

Indominus rex's roar is estimated to reach 160 DB, that's as loud as a Boeing 747 airplane taking off.

DNA MYSTERY

At first, dino trainer Owen Grady is unsure as to what DNA has been used to create the aggressive Indominus rex, but he soon discovers she is part Raptor and that InGen has sinister intentions to use her as a military weapon.

Indominus rex™

Lives:	Now, in Jurassic World
Eats:	meat (and siblings!)
Length:	15.2 m long
Speed:	up to 45 km/h
Movie sightings:	*Jurassic World*

You are here:

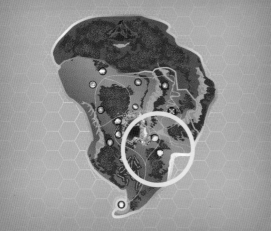

BIG BITE

Indominus rex's teeth are being constantly replaced, which is a genetic distinction common to all Theropods as well as nearly all sharks.

ACTIVATION PAGE

Release the terrifying **Indominus rex** with your mobile device by opening the app and viewing these pages.

Deadly Foe

Indominus rex is as clever as she is deadly. She sets out to trick her captors, escaping her paddock to roam free in Jurassic World.

The control room is stunned when they realize she's dug out her tracker so she can't be found.

When the paddock door is opened, Indominus rex races to freedom and embarks on a deadly hunting spree, causing carnage throughout Jurassic World.

Revealing a sharp mind, Idominus rex baffles her keepers by scratching her paddock wall to make it look as if she has escaped.